A Dangerous Weekend

I Talk You Talk Press

CONTENTS

1. WEDNESDAY

My name is Kirstie Brooks. I am English, but I live in Austria in a city called Graz. I am a secretary. I work for a lawyer. Last Wednesday, I was very happy. My boyfriend Heinrich called. He said his mother was coming to Graz, and she wanted to meet me. Heinrich is a lawyer for another company. We started dating about six months ago. We planned our first holiday together for Easter. Easter Monday is a public holiday in Austria. My company and Heinrich's company are closed on Good Friday too, so we could go away for four days. I thought Heinrich was getting serious about our relationship because he was taking me to stay with his grandmother. Now his mother wanted to meet me too! I started thinking about engagement rings and weddings.

On Wednesday afternoon, I asked my boss if I could go home a little early. I wanted to look my best when I met Heinrich's mother. I am very tall and thin. I hate to wear dresses or skirts, but I put on a simple dark blue dress, and the pearl necklace and earrings I was given by my grandmother. And flat shoes of course. Heinrich is shorter than me. He doesn't like me to wear high heels. He says it makes him look stupid.

I did my hair and make-up very carefully, put on my best coat and went out to wait for the bus.

The restaurant was in a very expensive hotel in the middle of town. I arrived late. Heinrich and his mother were waiting in the hotel lounge.

Heinrich introduced me to his mother. She looked at her watch.

"You're late," she said.

1

"I'm sorry. The bus took longer than I thought. But I am very pleased to meet you," I said nervously.

"There is no time for a drink before dinner," she answered. "We must go to our table now."

The dining room was very formal. The tables were set with silver knives, forks and spoons, and crystal glasses. The food was delicious, but the evening was terrible. Heinrich's mother asked me about my family.

"What is your father's job?" she asked.

"He has a small bookshop in my hometown. My mother works in the shop too."

"What university did you go to? Did you study German at university?"

"I never went to university," I answered. "I went to secretarial school. I got a job in an office. I liked German at high school, so I did a lot of courses by distance learning."

"Now I understand why you do not have a good German accent," she said.

After that, she didn't talk to me. She talked to Heinrich about family friends and relatives. I tried hard to be friendly, but I was sure she didn't like me.

We left the restaurant at 10:00pm. Heinrich spoke to the man at the front desk.

"Please tell the car park staff to bring my car now."

We walked out onto the hotel steps.

"Good night," I said to Heinrich's mother. "It was a pleasure to meet you."

"I hope you enjoyed yourself," she answered. "It is one of the best restaurants in Graz."

"Thank you for the lovely meal, Heinrich," I said. "I'll see you tomorrow."

"Yes," said Heinrich. "See you tomorrow." He turned to talk to his mother. "Mother, are you cold? Would you like to wait inside until the car comes?"

I walked down the steps and along the street to the bus stop. I felt very depressed. *That was not a success,* I thought. *Heinrich's mother doesn't like me.*

When I got home I changed into my favourite pyjamas and made myself a cup of hot chocolate. I turned on my music player and sat on the sofa. I started to feel more cheerful.

Heinrich is thirty years old, I thought. *It's OK if his mother doesn't like me. He is not a child. We are going on holiday on Friday. We will stay with his grandmother. I am sure she will like me, and I will like her.*

2. THURSDAY

Heinrich and I ate lunch together every Thursday. We always went to a nice sandwich and coffee bar near the park. That Thursday, I was ten minutes early.

His mother was angry last night because I was late, I thought. *I will show Heinrich that I can be early.*

I was surprised when I arrived. Heinrich was already sitting at our usual table.

I sat down at the table and held his hand.

"Hi!" I said. "Tomorrow, we'll be on holiday. What time will we leave? I checked on Google maps. It will take six hours to drive to your grandmother's house. What time does she expect us?"

Heinrich pulled his hand away. "We're not going."

"What!" I said loudly.

"Well, I'm going. But you are not invited now. My mother doesn't think you will be a good wife. She says wives must be useful for their husbands' careers. She says you are the wrong person for me."

"Heinrich! You are thirty years old! Why do you care what your mother thinks? You shouldn't listen to her!"

Heinrich didn't answer. He picked up the menu and looked at it. Then he put it down, and looked at me.

"My grandmother knows some very rich and powerful people. My mother called her this morning. She asked my grandmother to talk to her friends. She wants my grandmother to introduce me to some nice girls from good families."

I was very angry. I stood up and shouted at him. "My family is no good?"

Heinrich's face went red.

"Sit down, Kirstie. People are looking at us. I am sure your parents are very nice people. But they won't help my career. I need a wife who will help me become rich and powerful. You can't help me."

I picked up my bag and walked out of the restaurant. I ran across the street and into the park. I was so angry! I was shaking. I walked very fast through the park. I didn't look where I was going. I walked in front of an old man on a bicycle. He tried to stop, and fell off his bicycle onto the ground.

"Oh! I am so sorry. I wasn't looking properly," I said as I picked up his bicycle.

"It's OK. I am not hurt," he said. He seemed to be a nice man. He looked at me. "But are you OK? You look very upset."

"No! I am not OK! I am very angry," I answered.

The man looked at me and smiled. "Boyfriend trouble?"

"Yes!"

The man patted my arm.

"Why don't you go to the duck pond? You can sit in the sun and watch the ducks. It will make you feel better."

I made sure that he was OK. I stood and watched as he got back on his bicycle, and rode away. He waved and shouted, "Duck pond!" as he disappeared through the trees.

I walked to the duck pond and sat down. The old man was right. After a few minutes I felt much better.

I took out my smartphone and called my boss.

"I am very sorry. I have a terrible headache," I said. "I want to go home and lie down."

"I am sorry you are ill," said my boss. "Go home and go to bed. You must be well tomorrow, so that you can enjoy your holiday. See you on Tuesday!"

I walked back to the busy street to find a bus. I felt very strange. An hour ago I had a boyfriend. I was dreaming of marriage. I was going on holiday for four days. Now I was telling lies to my boss. I was going home in the middle of the day to an empty apartment. I had no boyfriend, no dreams, and no holiday plans.

I got off the bus and walked down the street towards my apartment. It is in a big old house. The owner divided the house into five small apartments. I love my apartment. It is on the second floor. There are wooden steps to a balcony and my front door opens onto the balcony.

Can I stay here in Graz? I will see Heinrich everywhere. His office is close to my office. He comes for meetings at my company. Maybe I should change jobs. Maybe I should go back to England. I felt very angry again. *Heinrich is a rat! He has ruined my life!*

I ran up the steps to my balcony, and put my hand in my bag to take out the key. No key! I sat down on the steps and emptied my bag. There was no key. Where was it? Then I remembered – my desk keys are on the same ring as my house key. My key ring was sitting on my desk at work. My boss thought I was ill. My boss did not expect to see me until Tuesday.

I put everything back into my bag, and put my head in my hands. I wanted to cry. Everything was going wrong. It was a terrible day.

3. OTTER

"Move over," said a voice.

I was surprised.

"Move over, so I can sit down," said the voice again.

I lifted my head and looked up. It was Otter. Otter lives in the apartment downstairs. Otter is not his real name. The name on the mailbox for his apartment says 'John Smith'. Otter says this is a joke. But if you ask him his real name, he always says, "Just call me Otter."

Otter wears jeans everywhere. He rides a motorbike. He is often out all night. I think he has many part-time jobs. Once I saw him serving in a grocery shop, and another time I saw him working at the fish market. He is very friendly, but he doesn't talk about himself. Today I was very pleased to see him.

I moved over, and Otter sat down on the step next to me.

"You look terrible," he said.

I looked at Otter. "You look terrible too!" Otter always looks very casual and untidy, but today he looked worse. His hair needed a cut. It also needed a wash. He hadn't had a shave for days, and his clothes were very dirty.

"You smell bad too!" I said.

Otter laughed. He held his arm up to his nose. "Mmmm. Rotten fish! I have a good reason for looking terrible. But why do you look so bad? Your face is all red, and you look very tired. You are home in the middle of the day. What's wrong?"

"It's a bad day," I answered.

Otter smiled. "Tell me about it."

I told Otter about Heinrich, and Heinrich's mother, and the holiday. I told him about my key ring.

"Everything's wrong! I can't get into my apartment! I am so upset and so angry!"

Then I started to cry. Once I started crying I couldn't stop. Otter didn't say anything. He searched in my bag and found a packet of tissues. He gave them to me. Finally I couldn't cry any more.

"Heinrich is an idiot," said Otter. "I can't fix your love life, but I can help with the keys and the holiday."

"How?"

"Well, first, I can open your door."

"How?"

"I have keys to all the apartments in this house."

"Why?" I was very surprised. The owner of the building lives in Vienna. I thought he might have given spare keys to someone. But Otter seemed so casual and crazy. Why did he give the keys to Otter and not to the retired doctor who lived upstairs?

"If you can open the door for me and lend me the extra key, that would be wonderful," I said.

Otter stood up. "Wait here."

He walked down the steps and went into his apartment. He soon came back with a key. "There you are. Don't lose it."

"Thank you." I stood up and went to my apartment door.

"Are you sure you are OK?" asked Otter.

"I'll be fine, thank you." I wanted to get inside and be alone. I wanted to have a shower and wash my hair.

"OK." Otter turned to walk down the steps. "I'll be back later."

"What for?"

"To fix your second problem. Four days' holiday. Nowhere to go, and nothing to do! I can fix that too."

4. OTTER HAS A PLAN

It was after 7:00pm when Otter came back. I was cooking spaghetti when I heard the doorbell ring. I looked out the side window and saw him. He had showered and shaved and changed his clothes. He looked a lot cleaner.

Otter said he had an idea for my holiday. *Something crazy I guess. Maybe he wants me to work at the fish market. I hope he smells better now, than he did this afternoon!*

I unlocked the door. "Come in. I am cooking spaghetti. Do you want some?"

Otter walked through into the kitchen. "Smells good. I'm surprised you are cooking. I thought you would be too heartbroken to eat."

"I'm surprised too. My heart is broken, but my stomach is fine. I like to cook, and I am very hungry. I didn't eat lunch," I said. "Do you want to eat?"

"Yes. I'd like to eat spaghetti with you. But first I'll go downstairs and get a bottle of wine."

"That's not necessary," I said. "I don't need wine."

Otter laughed. "I want to tell you my plan for the holiday weekend. I think it will be easier if you drink some wine first!"

He went out and I thought, *Yes! Otter has some mad plan. I hope it has nothing to do with the fish market! I am happy to give him some of my spaghetti. He was very kind to me this afternoon, but I won't do anything with him this weekend. I am not crazy!*

I put salad and spaghetti and meat sauce on the table. I found two wine glasses and a bottle opener. Otter soon came back with a bottle of Chianti.

"Perfect for spaghetti!" he smiled as he opened the bottle and filled the glasses.

I enjoyed eating with Otter. We talked about music and food. Otter told funny stories about working as a waiter. The time passed quickly.

Otter poured the last of the wine into my glass and said, "Now, holiday plans. I'm going to Wiesing. It's a beautiful town near Innsbruck. The house is large, and there is a housekeeper. You can come with me. She will cook all the meals, or we can go to bars, or to restaurants. We can go to the Easter festival in Innsbruck. It will be great."

"Otter?"

"Yes?"

"Why do you want me to go with you?"

"Uh. Well. The truth is …"

"Yes?"

"My sister lives there. It's my sister's house. She is married to a bank manager. His hobby is playing the trumpet. He plays the trumpet in a brass band. The band is going to play in a music festival in Liechtenstein. She wants to go with him, but she has two children. She doesn't want to take the children with her. The housekeeper will be there most of the time, but she doesn't want to leave the children with only the housekeeper. She wants me to go and stay there. To look after the children. Come with me. It will be fun!"

I laughed. "So this is your idea of a perfect Easter holiday for me. Go with you into the mountains, and spend the weekend looking after children! How old are they?"

"Mmmm. I am not sure. I don't think they go to school."

"Not babies! I am not looking after babies!"

"No! No! They walk. I am sure they walk."

"Otter! These children are your nieces or nephews. You must know something about them!"

Otter looked pleased. "Their names. I know their names. They are called Anabel and Jaime. They are lovely children. My sister says they are very good children."

I got up from the table and started making coffee. I wanted to think.

Do I want to go with Otter? No. Not really. But if I stay in Graz I will be very lonely. Most of my friends will be away. I have very little money, because I spent so much on new clothes for the visit to Heinrich's grandmother.

I took the coffee over to the table and poured a cup for Otter.

"What will you do if you stay here?" he asked. "Looking after children with me will be more fun than sitting here with a broken heart."

"You're right. I will come. When do we leave?"

"Tomorrow about three o'clock."

"I'll be ready," I said.

Otter drank his coffee. He stood up.

"Thank you for the meal. It was delicious. I'll be busy tomorrow morning, but I'll be back here tomorrow afternoon."

"OK. Goodnight," I said. I walked with him to the door. As I watched him going down the steps, I remembered to ask him something.

"Otter!" I called. "How are we getting to Wiesing?"

He stopped, and looked back up the steps.

"On my motorbike of course! Wear warm clothes and only bring a small travel bag."

He disappeared, and I went back inside and shut the apartment door loudly.

I am crazy, I thought. *Why am I doing this?*

I cleaned up in the kitchen and went to bed. I fell asleep easily, but then I woke up around 3:00am. I lay in my bed sweating.

I am going away with Otter, on a motorbike, into the mountains. I don't know his real name. I don't know how old he is, or where he comes from. He always speaks to me in English. His English doesn't sound American or British. I know he speaks German very well. Where was he born? I know nothing about him. I must be crazy.

I lay awake and worried for a long time, but finally, I fell asleep again.

5. FRIDAY

I slept late. When I climbed out of bed and went to the window, I saw the weather was beautiful. It was quite cold, but the sky was blue and there was no wind. I packed a small backpack with toiletries and extra clothes. I found my heavy winter jacket, leather gloves, and a warm scarf. I planned to wear my walking boots for travelling on the motorbike. Then I cleaned my apartment. I was taking a bag of garbage down to the garbage storage area when I saw Erika Stringbaum. Erika was a doctor, but she retired a long time ago. She is a tiny woman with beautiful white hair and bright brown eyes. Her hobby is gardening. She looks after the garden around the house. She grows flowers and vegetables. She gives vegetables to everyone who lives in the house. She often knocks on my door with a bag of carrots, or tomatoes, or a cabbage.

Erika was kneeling on the ground. She was tidying the garden. I walked over to talk to her.

"Good morning, Erika. It's a lovely day isn't it?"

She looked up and smiled. "Kirstie! How nice to see you. Yes it is a lovely day. What are your plans for the holiday weekend?"

"Uh. I'm going to Wiesing with Otter. He has to look after his sister's children. He asked me to go and help him," I said. I wondered what Erika would say. I thought, *If Erika says it is a bad idea, then I won't go.*

But Erika said, "That's nice. Wiesing is so pretty. You will enjoy it."

"Erika? Where does Otter come from? What nationality is he?"

"I don't think about it," answered Erika. "I think of him as an international man."

"Do you know his real name?" I asked.

"I always call him Otter," Erika answered. "It seems to be a good name for him."

I said goodbye to Erika, and went back inside. Erika didn't think it was a strange idea for me to go away with Otter, so I decided not to worry anymore.

Just before 3:00pm I heard Otter's motorbike outside. I went to the doorway and looked down.

"Hurry up! It's time to leave," shouted Otter when he saw me. He was wearing his leather jacket, helmet and goggles.

I put on my heavy jacket, scarf and gloves and picked up my backpack. I locked the door and ran down to the motorbike. He tied my backpack to the back of the motorbike. He handed a helmet to me. I put it on, and climbed onto the back of the motorbike.

It took about five hours to get to Wiesing. I was cold and stiff when we arrived. We stopped outside the church.

"The house is down that street," said Otter. He pointed to a side street. He got off the bike and untied my backpack. He handed it to me and said, "The house is number seventeen. Wait outside. I'm going to find somewhere to put the bike."

I walked slowly across the road and into the side street. Number 17 was a tall house with flower baskets hanging from the top floors. There were steps from the street up to a heavy wooden door. I sat on the steps and waited for Otter. I waited there for 15 minutes. Then the door opened.

"Come in!" said Otter. "The children are already in bed. You can meet them in the morning."

I walked into the wide hall. An elderly woman, dressed in a dark blue dress and an apron, was standing at the bottom of the stairs.

"Kirstie, this is Frau Kruger. She has a meal ready for us."

I shook hands with Frau Kruger.

"Did you have a good trip?" Frau Kruger asked. "I am so pleased you are here. The children are very good, but it is not my job to look after them. My job is to clean and cook. And on Sunday, I am going to visit my sister in Maurach. I won't come back until Monday. I was so pleased when Herr Schmitt telephoned to say you were coming."

This is a bit strange, I thought. *Why didn't Otter's sister tell her he was coming?*

I turned to look at Otter and had another surprise. He looked very neat and handsome. His hair was shorter, he had shaved, and he was wearing smart and expensive casual clothes.

"Where did you get those clothes?" I whispered to him.

"I am the brother-in-law of a bank manager. I have to look smart and rich," he answered softly.

"Come upstairs," said Frau Kruger. "I will show you your bedroom."

Otter picked up my backpack and his bag, and we followed Frau Kruger up the steep stairway.

I was worried. *Bedroom? What does she mean 'bedroom'? I hope she means 'bedrooms' or I am in big trouble!*

Frau Kruger stopped on the second floor landing. "Come this way," she said. "The little angels sleep in this room."

She opened the door to a bedroom. We looked in. I could see a cot and bed. There were boxes of toys along the wall.

"They are sleeping well," said Frau Kruger, and closed the door softly. She opened the door opposite the children's room.

"I prepared this room for you."

I walked into the room. It had a large bed with big pillows and a quilt. Everything was white cotton.

"The house has central heating, so you should be warm," said Frau Kruger.

"It looks very nice," said Otter. "I am sure we will be very comfortable."

"Frau Kruger? Where is my....Ouch!" I didn't finish speaking, because Otter stood on my foot. It hurt.

He put his face next to my ear and said, "Later!" very softly.

Frau Kruger was looking puzzled.

"Kirstie wants to know where you sleep," said Otter.

"Oh. I sleep upstairs. I have a nice bedroom, and a bathroom and a living room. Now please come downstairs to the dining room. I will serve your meal."

The dining room table was set for two people. Frau Kruger cooked mushroom soup, salmon and potatoes with a salad. The food was delicious.

Finally she brought a pot of coffee and a plate of little chocolate cakes into the room.

"I am going to bed now," she said. "I will see you in the morning."

"Thank you for the wonderful meal," I said. "Good night!"

"Good night, and thank you," said Otter.

I stood up and went to the dining room door. I listened as Frau Kruger climbed up the stairs. When I was sure she couldn't hear, I said, "Otter! She thinks we are married! What did you say?"

Otter laughed and poured himself some more wine. "Have some coffee, or some more wine. Relax!"

"Otter! If you don't tell me the truth, I am going to go upstairs and tell Frau Kruger your name is not Johan Schmitt, and we are not married!"

"Kirstie. Sit down and relax. Frau Kruger is a very religious woman. I didn't want to shock her. I told her you and I were staying here. Of course she thought you were my wife."

"OK. But where are you sleeping tonight? You are not sleeping in the bedroom with me!"

"Don't worry. I'll find somewhere to sleep," answered Otter. "But don't talk so loudly. You will wake the children."

I drank a coffee and ate two of the little chocolate cakes. Otter was very quiet. I thought he was listening for something. I looked at the old-fashioned clock on the wall. It was only 10:30pm, but I was very tired.

"I'm going to bed," I said. "Do you want some coffee?"

"Yes. Leave the coffee pot. Sleep well."

"See you in the morning, then," I said. I took my cup and plate out to the kitchen. It was very clean and tidy. The dishes and pots were all washed and put away. Frau Kruger was a good housekeeper. I washed my coffee cup and plate, and put them away. Then I walked slowly up the stairs and went to bed.

6. SATURDAY

It was almost 8:30am when I woke up. The room was quiet. The sunlight was coming into the room through the window. The bed was so warm and so comfortable, I didn't want to get up. I lay back on the pillows and watched little white clouds moving across the blue sky.

Wait a minute! The curtains were closed when I went to bed! Someone has been in here. Frau Kruger? Otter?

The thought made me feel strange. I got up, and took clean clothes from my backpack. Otter's bag was on the floor next to my backpack. I took a shower in the old-fashioned bathroom along the hallway. As I walked past the children's room, I looked in. The room was empty and the beds were made.

Down in the kitchen, the children were sitting at the table.

"Anabel! Jaime! This is your Aunty Kirstie," said Frau Kruger.

She looked very happy this morning. She was dressed casually in a sweater and skirt. Near the door from the kitchen to the back garden, was a suitcase. On top of the suitcase were a hat, and a heavy wool coat.

"Your husband is so kind!" said Frau Kruger. He told me I could take a holiday today. I can spend more time with my sister. He has gone to get the car! He will drive me to my sister's house."

"Uh. That's very nice. I hope you have a great time." I was panicking.

I don't know anything about children. What do they eat? What am I going to do?

Frau Kruger noticed I looked worried. "Don't worry," she said. "Jaime and Anabel are good children. You will have no trouble. I made boiled beef and vegetables yesterday. You can eat that tonight.

"Your husband said you are going to the Easter Festival in Innsbruck today. The children will need their warm jackets. Anabel's pushchair is in the cupboard under the stairs. Take Anabel's pink rabbit. She will go to sleep in her pushchair when she is tired, but she likes to have her rabbit."

Frau Kruger smiled at me. She put on her coat and hat and picked up the suitcase.

"Frau Kruger?" I said.

She turned to look at me. "Yes?"

"When will the children's mother and father come back from the music festival?"

Frau Kruger looked at me strangely. "There is no Herr Lang. Frau Lang said he died two years ago. Frau Lang has gone to Munich to look after her mother."

"Oh, I see. Did she say when she would come back?"

"She didn't say anything to me. We didn't talk about it. On Wednesday, I took the children on the bus to spend the day with my sister. When I came back, Frau Lang had gone. She left a note on the table for me."

"Are we ready, Frau Kruger?" Otter came into the kitchen. He took the suitcase from Frau Kruger. "Come along," he said.

As they walked out the kitchen door, he turned and spoke to me. "I'll be back in about forty-five minutes. We should leave for Innsbruck soon after that. Can you have the children ready please?"

He smiled and walked out, closing the door behind him.

I was very angry. Otter had given Frau Kruger an extra day's holiday. He was driving her to her sister's house. I was alone in the house with two small children!

I turned to look at the children. Jaime was eating bread. His face was covered in jam. He smiled at me. Anabel was staring at me. Her cup of milk was on its side and there was milk all over the table. Then she started to cry.

"Mama! Where's Mama?"

Poor little things, I thought. *Their mother isn't here. Even Frau Kruger has gone. They are alone in the house with a strange woman.*

I rushed to the table and picked Anabel up. I hugged her.

17

"It's OK. Mama will come back soon. We will go to the festival. We will have a wonderful day."

After a while Anabel stopped crying. "Drink," she said.

I sat her down at the table and gave her some more milk.

I cleared up the spilt milk and breadcrumbs. I cleaned Jaime's face, and told him to go to the bathroom.

"Uncle Johan will be back soon. We will go to Innsbruck. Maybe you can have a hot dog. Do you like hot dogs?"

"Hamburgers," answered Jaime. "I like hamburgers."

"OK," I said. "I will buy you a hamburger, and an ice cream in Innsbruck."

When Otter returned from Maurach, we were almost ready to leave. Jaime was sitting on the bottom step and I was tying his shoe laces. Anabel was sitting beside him holding a pink rabbit. I had warm jackets, hats, drink bottles, paper towels and tissues in my backpack.

"Anabel's pushchair is in the cupboard under the stairs. Can you get it and put it in the car please?"

"Sure," said Otter.

"And Otter?"

"Yes?"

"Where did the car come from?" I asked.

"It's my sister's car," answered Otter.

He took the pushchair from the cupboard and carried it out towards the kitchen. He soon came back. He picked up Anabel. I took Jaime's hand, and the backpack. I checked the front door was locked, and Jaime and I went through the kitchen and out the back door. Otter locked the back door with a big old-fashioned key. Then we followed him down the garden. There was a gate at the end of the garden and we stopped at a car parked in the back street.

I was sure that it was the children's mother's car. There were car seats for the children, and a small pile of children's books and toys on the back seat.

When the children were strapped into their car seats, I climbed into the front passenger seat next to Otter.

"You have a lot of questions to answer!" I said to him. "I want the truth!"

He laughed. "Later, Kirstie. Later. Let's have a great day out."

He is so annoying, I thought. *He never tells me the truth. What will today be like? I am sure he will disappear. I will be alone with the children all day.*

7. INNSBRUCK

We had a great time in Innsbruck. The children were too young for concerts, but there was a food market, street entertainers and a puppet show. The children laughed and shouted. They loved the puppets. So did I. Otter was very good with the children. He played with the children and made them laugh. He pushed Anabel's pushchair. He carried Jaime on his shoulders, when Jaime got tired.

By 4:00pm, I was tired, and so were the children. We found a small café, and sat outside eating ice cream. I enjoyed watching all the people walking in the street. The town was full. Not just local people, but many tourists had come for the festival.

Then Jaime pulled at my hand.

"That man has a big silver car," he said.

"What man?" I asked. Jaime pointed to a man sitting at a table near ours.

"That man," he said. "His car is silver. It is very big."

"How do you know?" I asked.

"I saw it. It was outside our house. That man was the driver."

"When did you see it?"

"In the morning. The day we went on the bus. The day Mama went away."

I turned to look at Otter, but he was gone. I didn't see him go. I didn't hear him go, but there was an empty seat.

He must have gone to the bathroom, I thought. *Isn't Jaime clever? He can remember a car and a driver.*

Anabel was falling asleep, so I put her into her pushchair with her rabbit. We finished our ice cream. The man at the other table, the man with the silver car, seemed to be watching us. I felt nervous.

"Let's go to the bathroom," I said to Jaime. "We will be going home soon."

I picked up Anabel. She was holding her rabbit and she was almost asleep.

The bathrooms were at the back of the café. I carried Anabel through the café. Jaime followed me closely.

The door to the men's bathroom was wide open. It seemed to be empty. A window at the back of the room was open. Outside I could see some garbage cans.

Where was Otter?

I took the children into the women's bathroom and locked the door. I opened the window and looked out. A chef walked out of a door at the back of the café to have a cigarette, but I couldn't see Otter.

I helped the children use the bathroom, and cleaned the ice cream off their faces and hands.

We walked back into the café. I looked through the window at our table. Otter wasn't there. I looked over to where the man with the silver car was sitting. He was talking on his mobile phone.

I felt nervous and worried.

Something is wrong, I thought. *Are the children in danger? Why do I think that? I'm thinking like that, because there seem to be many secrets. Otter has not told me the truth. I don't think these are his sister's children. Who are they? Where are their mother and father?*

I panicked. I picked up Anabel.

"We'll go to the car now," I said to Jaime. "Stay close to me."

I pushed past the woman at the cash desk and into the kitchen. The back door was open.

"You can't come in here!" said one of the cooks.

"Sorry," I said as I hurried through the kitchen and out the door.

I put Anabel on my hip so I could hold Jaime's hand. I held it tightly as we ran past the garbage cans into a narrow alley and out onto the busy street.

When we were in the middle of the crowd, I felt better. I looked down at Jaime. His face was red.

"I'm sorry, Jaime," I said. "We won't run anymore. We will walk slowly to the car. Can you do that?"

"OK," he said.

It took us a long time to walk to the parking garage. Anabel was heavy, and I got tired. Jaime was tired too. He couldn't walk fast.

Finally we saw the parking garage.

"Where is Uncle Johan?" asked Jaime.

"I don't know," I answered. "I think he will come soon."

"I want him now!"

We stopped walking. I knelt down and looked at Jaime. He had tears in his eyes.

"Why do you want Uncle Johan?" I asked.

"He drives the car," said Jaime.

"It's OK, Jaime," I said. "I can drive."

"But how will Uncle Johan get home?"

I didn't answer Jaime. I had remembered something important.

I am such an idiot! Otter has the car keys! Now what? The children and I can't even wait in the car. The doors are locked.

I looked around. The parking garages were outside the centre of the city. There were not so many people around. It was getting colder. I saw a narrow door with a sign that said *Bar-Live Music*.

A bar is not a good place to take small children, I thought. *But it will be quiet at this time on a Saturday afternoon. I will ask them if they can make a warm drink for the children.*

The bar was almost empty. The woman behind the bar was very kind. She took Anabel from me and carried her to a bench seat in a quiet corner. Jaime climbed onto the seat beside Anabel. The woman promised hot milk for the children and a coffee for me. I sat down on a seat opposite the children. I took out my smartphone and called Otter. He didn't answer his phone. I sent a text message. I explained how to find the bar. I asked him to come.

Then we waited. The children were too tired to drink their milk. They soon fell asleep. I drank my coffee and thought about the day.

Why did I panic? It was really crazy to run away. It was crazy to leave Anabel's pushchair outside on the street. It was crazy to run out through the kitchen door. Jaime is only a little boy. Maybe the man with the silver car was Jaime's imagination. But why did Otter disappear?

It was only a short time before Otter came into the bar. He spoke to the woman behind the bar and paid her. He came to the table and lifted Anabel up and gave her to me. Then he picked up Jaime. They were still sleeping. We walked across the road to the parking garage.

Ten minutes later, we were on the road back towards Wiesing. The children were asleep in their safety seats. Otter was very quiet. He didn't speak at all. I felt uncomfortable.

Maybe he is angry with me, I thought.

"I'm sorry I left Anabel's pushchair in the café," I said. "I was stupid. I don't know why I panicked and ran away."

"I have the pushchair. It is in the boot of the car," answered Otter.

"Oh," I said. "So you went back to the café?"

"Of course I did!" Otter sounded angry.

He didn't say anything more.

I tried again. "Thank you for coming to the bar so quickly," I said. "You must have hurried after you got my text message."

"I didn't need your text message," answered Otter. "I knew where you were."

"How did you know?"

"I put a GPS tracking app on your phone."

"What!" I shouted.

"Shhh," said Otter. "Don't shout. You'll wake the children."

I was so angry with Otter, I didn't say another word.

8. SATURDAY NIGHT

When we arrived in Wiesing, Otter parked the car in the back street about 100m from the house, and said, "Wait here."

He went along the street, and disappeared. I sat in the car with the children. After about ten minutes Otter came back.

"Everything seems OK," he said. He drove along the street to the gate at the back of the garden.

"We can take the children into the house."

It was an hour before Otter and I could sit down and eat a meal. I took the children to the bathroom and then dressed them in their pyjamas. Anabel was too tired to eat much, but I gave her some hot milk and a piece of bread. Jaime drank some of Frau Kruger's beef and vegetable soup. Otter and I carried them upstairs and put them into bed. I stayed in the children's room until they fell asleep. Then I went down and joined Otter in the dining room. He had set the table and opened a bottle of wine. The beef and vegetable soup was in a big dish on the table.

Suddenly, I felt very hungry. We ate Frau Kruger's delicious cooking, and drank some wine.

"Now Otter!" I said. "I want to know now! Tell me the truth."

"Just a minute," he said. He got up from the table and went out. I could hear him moving around the house. When he came back he said, "No one is here. I think it's safe."

He sat down again and picked up his wine glass.

"Talk!" I shouted.

"OK, OK. I'll tell you."

"At last," I said. "The truth."

"Well, the children's father was a bank manager."

"But he is not your brother-in-law?" I asked.

"No. But he was the manager of a small bank in Vienna. Late last year, the bank was robbed. It was almost closing time, and there were no customers when the bank robbers came in. They were wearing masks. They had guns. One of the bank tellers was very brave, but crazy. He jumped at one of the bank robbers and pulled the mask off. The robbers killed him. They killed the other bank teller too. The children's father was hurt. He was very ill for a long time, but he lived. He is still in hospital.

"The police think they know who robbed the bank. They have the two men in prison, but they need proof. The children's father can identify one of the men. The police need his identification. But the bank robbers come from a very powerful gang of criminals. Everyone was very worried about the safety of the bank manager's wife and children. The police thought the gang might kidnap them. Then the father would not help the police, in case the gang members killed his family.

"His wife brought the children here to this house to hide. It is far from Vienna, and we thought she would be safe. She used a different name. She said her name was Gerta Lang. Everything was fine. Next week, her husband will leave the hospital. There will be a court case, and everything will be over. But on Wednesday, Gerta Lang disappeared. We think she was kidnapped, but there have been no messages from the gang.

"My job was to come here and protect the children. Also to watch and listen. Maybe some members of the gang are still in the area. Maybe a message will come to this house."

"So who left the letter for Frau Kruger? The letter saying Gerta Lang had gone to Munich to look after her mother?" I asked.

"I did," said Otter. "I came here on Wednesday. I didn't want Frau Kruger to think anything was strange. I wrote the letter. It was a busy day. I had to go back to my night job in Graz."

"Something with fish?" I asked.

Otter laughed. "Yes, something with fish."

"Otter?" I said.

"Yes?" he answered.

"What is your job? What do you do?"

Maybe Otter is a policeman, I thought.

"That's complicated. One day I will tell you," said Otter. "Do you want some coffee, or a cup of tea?"

"Tea, please," I answered.

When Otter came back from the kitchen with the tea, I had another question.

"What happened today in Innsbruck? Was there real danger?"

Otter looked serious. "I don't know. But maybe, yes. It was a good thing you took the children away."

"Why did you disappear?"

"I saw a man in that café. I knew he was a member of the gang. I didn't want him to see me. So I disappeared for a while. When I came back, you and the children were gone. I was so worried. I thought you were kidnapped. I was angry with myself. My job was to keep the children safe. But the café staff told me what you did. I knew you ran away. That was very smart."

"So the man with the silver car was a gang member?" I asked.

"What man with the silver car?" Otter looked puzzled.

"When we were in the café, Jaime recognized a man at another table. He said that the man had a big silver car. He said he saw the man here in Wiesing when they got off the bus from Maurach. The day his mother left."

"That's interesting. Why didn't you tell me?" Otter stood up quickly.

"I tried to tell you, but you had gone. You just disappeared. Remember? That's when I started to get nervous."

Otter wasn't listening to me. He was talking to someone on his phone.

"Yes. He was seen here in Wiesing. He was driving a big silver car. .... I think it is true. The boy saw him...... Yes, he is very young. .....Yes, he could make a mistake, but I don't think so. I saw him too, in Innsbruck......

"I need some help. When can you send some extra people? .... What! That's too late! Please try to send someone sooner."

Otter put his phone in his pocket and turned to me.

"Go to bed, Kirstie. Try to get some sleep. Tomorrow might be a busy day."

I was too tired to ask any more questions. I was too tired to argue with Otter.

"OK," I said. "Good night."

As I walked past Otter, he touched my face gently. "You did well today," he said softly.

"Did I?" I yawned.

I went to the bathroom to wash, and to clean my teeth. I changed into my pyjamas, turned off the light, and climbed into the wide bed. I couldn't sleep. There was danger in this house. Otter hadn't said anything about danger here in Wiesing, but I knew he was worried.

I climbed out of bed and went to the children's room. Anabel was sleeping, but Jaime was awake. I picked Anabel up out of her bed and carried her into the big bedroom. I put her in the wide bed and went back for Jaime.

"Do you want to go to the bathroom?" I asked.

"Yes," he answered. I went with him to the bathroom, then took him to my bedroom. He climbed into the big bed, and immediately fell asleep. I joined the children in the bed. For a while I listened to the old house. It made the noises that all old houses make in the night. I thought I could hear Otter moving around downstairs.

Then I heard someone walking up the stairs. I was terrified. I put my arms around the sleeping children and waited.

The door opened. It was Otter.

"Are you OK?" he asked.

"Yes. Yes. I'm fine. But I want the children here. I am worried for them," I answered.

"It's a good idea," said Otter. "But don't worry. I'll make sure no one gets into the house tonight."

He smiled and closed the door. I heard him walking along the hallway and up the stairs towards Frau Kruger's room.

I thought I wouldn't be able to sleep, but I was wrong.

9. SUNDAY MORNING

When I woke up, the house was very quiet. The children were still sleeping. I took a shower, got dressed and went downstairs. Otter was not there. I looked at the clock on the dining room wall. It was 6:30am.

The dishes from our meal the night before were piled up on the kitchen counter. I put the coffee maker on. While I was waiting for the coffee, I washed and dried the dishes. I looked out of the window. It was a grey day. Far away, across the valley, I could see black clouds.

It will rain later, I thought. *Maybe we should take the children for a walk this morning, before the rain comes. We....? Where is Otter? I'm alone with the children again. Otter makes me so angry!*

The small garbage container in the kitchen was full. I pulled out the liner bag and tied it up. I planned to take it down to the garbage cans near the back gate.

When I opened the back door I got a surprise. There was a large basket on the step. It was decorated with rabbits and ribbons. It was full of small toys and chocolate eggs.

On top of the basket was a piece of paper with 'Kirstie' in large letters. I picked up the paper and read the message. It was from Otter.

---*'Do not open the door again! Do not let the children leave the house! Stay away from the windows.*

Happy Easter,

Love Otter'---

I picked up the basket and went back inside. I closed the door very loudly.

Otter is so annoying, I thought. *Where is he? What is he doing?*

I put the basket on the kitchen table, and poured myself a cup of coffee.

It's Easter Sunday! The children must be missing their mother. I must make today special for them.

Then I had a great idea.

I'll make an Easter egg hunt for them. I'll hide these eggs all over the house. I'll hide these little toys too. They can search for them.

I finished my coffee and took the basket from the table.

It took me a long time to hide the eggs and tiny toys. I put them in low places so that Anabel would be able to find them. I had just finished when Jaime appeared at the top of the stairs. He looked so young and unhappy.

"Anabel is crying," he said. "She wants Mama. I do too."

Oh, these poor children! It is not fair! I thought. I ran up the stairs and sat on the top step. I hugged Jaime.

"It's OK, Jaime," I said. "Mama will come back very soon. We will go get Anabel and then we will have breakfast."

Jaime and I sat on the bed, while I held Anabel. She wouldn't stop crying.

The pink rabbit! I thought. *She needs her rabbit.*

"Please find Anabel's rabbit," I said to Jaime. The little boy climbed off the bed and went back to their bedroom. He came back with the pink rabbit and gave it to Anabel. It was magic. She took the toy, and stopped crying.

It was after 9:00am before I had the children washed, dressed, and down in the kitchen. After breakfast, the children watched television while I cleaned the kitchen and made the beds.

I was opening the curtains in the children's room, when I remembered Otter's message - *Stay away from the windows!*

I've left the children alone downstairs! What if Jaime opens the door?

I raced downstairs. The children were sitting on the floor in the living room watching a cartoon on television.

I sat on the floor with my arms around the children until I felt calm again.

Where was Otter? What was happening?

After a while, Jaime got bored with watching television.

"Can we go out? I want to go out and play," he said.

"I have a surprise for you," I answered. "It is Easter Sunday, so we are going to have a treasure hunt."

The treasure hunt was a great success. The little chocolate eggs and toys were all over the house. The children were very excited. Anabel wanted to eat all the chocolate she found, but Jaime wanted to save his.

"I want to give some to Mama," he said.

I wanted to cry.

Poor little boy, I thought. *This is not fair. Where is his mother? Where is Otter?*

10. HIDING

I was sitting at the kitchen table watching Anabel and Jaime look for toys in a cupboard when Otter appeared.

"Where did you come from?" I shouted.

Otter knelt on the floor next to my chair. He put his finger against my lips.

"Shhhh. I only have a few minutes. The information about the big silver car was very useful. The police have looked at security cameras and traffic cameras all through the area. They have found the silver car. They think the children's mother was kidnapped. But they also think they know where the gang is keeping her. A team is going to rescue her. But we have a problem."

"We do?" I whispered. "What problem?"

"The gang planned to kidnap Gerta and the children last Wednesday. They didn't get the children because they were in Maurach with Frau Kruger. They still want to take the children. I asked for help. Erika promised to send a team, but they didn't arrive."

"Erika? Erika Stringbaum? I don't understand!"

"Shhh. Stop shouting!"

"I'm not shouting!" I was puzzled and angry.

"Yes you are. Now be quiet. I have to go. I'll explain more later."

Just as Otter stood up, there was a noise at the back of the house. I could see the shape of a man outside the kitchen door.

I looked at Otter. He had a gun in his hand.

"Run, Kirstie," said Otter. "Take the children upstairs! Hurry!"

I picked up Anabel from the floor. Somehow I picked up Jaime too. The children held onto me tightly as I ran towards the stairs.

When I got to the top of the house I felt dizzy. I couldn't breathe. I put the children on the floor outside Frau Kruger's bedroom. I leant against the bedroom door and waited for my heartbeat to return to normal.

I heard the sound of a gunshot. There were no voices, but I could hear bangs and then the sound of breaking glass.

How many men are there? Is Otter fighting one man or more? Do they have guns?

I opened the door to Frau Kruger's room. I picked Anabel up from the floor and put her on the bed. Jaime followed.

"We're not allowed to come in here," he said. "Mama says it's Frau Kruger's room and it's private."

"Today is special," I said. "Today we're playing a special game. We're hiding. So we must be very quiet."

I'm telling Jaime to be quiet, I thought. *But my heart is banging so loudly I am sure other people can hear it.*

I closed the door and stood behind it. I took deep breaths until I calmed down.

Jaime was bouncing up and down on the bed.

"Jaime. You must be very quiet. You mustn't make any noise."

I was listening hard. I couldn't hear any sounds. The house was old, and the door was made of strong wood.

I looked around the room. There was a big storage box in the corner. I dragged it across the floor and put it against the door. I looked around the room. I took the small table next to the bed and put it on top of the box.

Jaime was puzzled. "If Uncle Johan can't open the door, he can't find us. I don't like this game! I want to do more treasure hunting. Are there chocolates and toys in this room?"

Jaime climbed off the bed and crawled underneath it.

I heard loud sounds outside the door. Someone was trying to open it. I heard shouting. There was more than one man! I picked Anabel up and pushed her under the bed with Jaime. "Don't make a sound!" I whispered.

The table fell off the top of the box. The box was moving! In a few seconds they would push the door open. I ran to the window. There was a narrow balcony outside. I opened the window and climbed out.

I saw baskets of flowers hanging from the roof above the balcony. I heard bangs and crashes outside the door. Suddenly I was not frightened. I was very, very angry.

I climbed onto the railing of the balcony. I took one of the flower baskets and held it by the chain. And I waited.

There was shouting. "They went out the window!"

A man leant out of the window. I swung the basket as hard as I could and hit him on the head. He fell out of the window onto the floor of balcony. A second man appeared. He got out of the window and turned to hold me. I tried to hit him with the basket, but I missed. He took my arm. I dropped the basket and fell off the railing on top of him. Then I heard someone laughing.

"Kirstie! You are amazing!" Otter was at the window.

"Amazing? Amazing!" I was so angry. "Where were you? Those guys almost got the children!"

I tried to stand up. I wanted to hit Otter as hard as I could. Then I saw that his right arm was bleeding. He was holding his gun in his left hand. He was very pale.

"It's OK, Kirstie. Can you climb back through the window? I must watch these two."

I climbed back into the room.

"Kirstie? Can you find something to tie these guys up with?"

I looked in Frau Kruger's drawers. I found some scarves and belts. I took them to Otter. He was still pointing the gun at the two men. The man I fell on was sitting up. The man I hit with the basket was not moving.

"Did I kill him?" I asked.

"I hope so," answered Otter. "He is not a nice person. Hold the gun. I will tie them up. I know you are mad at me, but please don't shoot me."

"What about your arm?"

"It will be OK." It took Otter a few minutes, but he tied both men up so that they could not move.

Then he climbed back into the room and closed the window.

His arm was bleeding badly now. He smiled at me.

"I want some answers," I shouted.

"I know. But I am not going to answer your questions while you are holding a gun."

He held out his left hand and I gave him the gun.

"Can Uncle Johan find us now?" A voice came from under the bed.

"Oh, Jaime! Anabel! I'm so sorry!"

Otter and I got the children from under the bed, and we all went downstairs.

11. SUNDAY AFTERNOON

I gave the children milk and cookies, and turned the television on. Otter went outside and talked on his smartphone for a long time.

It was very quiet. I sat on a chair in the living room and watched the children. I didn't want to leave them. The few minutes upstairs had been terrifying. I didn't want to think about it.

Then suddenly the house was full of people – policemen, a doctor, men in suits who didn't say anything, a man in jeans taking photographs…

The doctor took Otter upstairs.

No one spoke to me, or to the children. At about 4:00pm a black car came down the street and stopped in front of the house. A blonde woman jumped out of the car and ran into the house.

"Jaime, Anabel!" she shouted.

"Mama!" shouted the children.

She was Gerta Lang. She was the children's mother. The police had tracked the silver car, and found Gerta locked in a barn near Innsbruck.

I went to the kitchen, and looked in the refrigerator. There was a lot of beef and vegetables left. I put the pot on the stove to heat and started peeling potatoes.

No one has eaten anything since breakfast, I thought. *I should make food.* I found bread and ham, and made sandwiches too. I found a big coffee pot.

"Time to go," said Otter. He was standing by the kitchen door. He had my bag and his bag in his hand.

"How's your arm?" I asked.

Otter said, "It's not serious. The bullet went through the flesh. It didn't hit any bones."

"Is that my bag?"

"Yes, I packed for you. It's time to go."

"Why?"

"If we go now, maybe no one will remember we were here," said Otter. "That would be good."

"But I'm hungry!"

Otter laughed. "I'll buy you a hamburger later."

"Did you get all my things?"

"Of course!"

"Did you check the bathroom?"

"Of course. Now can we please go? Some of those guys out there are looking at me. I think they want to talk. I don't want to talk to them."

I put down the coffee pot and took my bag from Otter. I followed him out the kitchen door and down the garden.

"But how can we get back to Graz?" I asked. "You can't ride your motorbike."

"No. But you can drive," he said. "I'll come back next week to get my motorbike."

In the back street behind the house was an Audi sports car. I was very surprised.

"We are going to drive back to Graz in that?"

"Why not?" asked Otter. He threw his bag into the back of the car, and climbed into the passenger seat.

I put my bag in the back too, and got into the driver's seat.

"Of course we can't arrive in Graz in such an expensive car," said Otter. "When we get near Graz, we'll leave this car and catch a bus!"

12. SOME ANSWERS

I loved driving the car. It was so powerful. I had never driven anything like it before. Otter went to sleep.

He probably got no sleep last night, I thought. *And he got shot. I am not surprised he's tired.*

Near Liezen Otter woke up.

"Let's eat," he said. I found a small hotel near the river, and parked outside.

We ordered hamburgers and coffee and went outside. We sat at one of the tables on the terrace. I ate my hamburger and drank half my coffee. Then I took a deep breath.

"Are you a policeman?" I asked.

"No. But I work for the police sometimes. I work for other people too."

"In Austria?"

"I work in other countries sometimes."

"Are you are private detective? Or are you a spy?"

Otter laughed. "No. I find things out. I go to places, and do things the police can't do."

"And what about Erika?"

"She's my boss."

"But she's a retired doctor!"

"Maybe. I don't know."

I drank some more coffee and thought about everything.

"How did the gangsters find out where Gerta and the children were hiding?" I asked.

"That was bad luck. There was a festival in Wiesing. Some photographs were in the newspaper. In one of the photographs, Anabel and her pink rabbit were at the front. The gangsters recognised her. Then it was easy for them to find the house."

"And why didn't the team arrive to help you? You said Erika promised to send some people."

"That was not good. They were driving very fast, and they had an accident. The driver is dead and the three passengers are in hospital."

"Oh, I am so sorry. That's terrible."

We sat for a long time without talking.

Then I said. "Otter? I have another question."

"No! No! Not more questions!" he laughed.

"This one's easy," I said.

"OK. Ask me. What do you want to know?"

"Where do you come from? You aren't Austrian are you?"

"No. I lived most of my life in Australia. My parents have a crocodile farm."

"Otter!" I shouted. "You make up so many stories. You tell so many lies!"

"Yes. I do. With my job you have to be good at lying. You have to be good at making up stories."

I felt unhappy. "It's a problem for me. I don't know when you are telling lies. I don't know what's true."

"OK. Let me ask you a question. If you answer it, I will tell you one true thing. I promise."

"Go ahead. Ask the question," I said.

"Did you think about Heinrich this weekend?"

I thought about it. I was so angry on Thursday and Friday. I told Otter I had a broken heart. But maybe I didn't. Maybe I was just angry. Maybe I didn't love Heinrich.

"Mmm. No. I didn't think about him at all on Saturday or today. I don't think I loved him. I don't think my heart is broken," I said.

"Good," said Otter. He stood up and moved around the table. He took my hand and smiled down at me.

"I promise this is true. Erika found someone to go with me to Wiesing, and help look after the children. But I said 'no'. I wanted you to go with me. It was the only way I could spend time with you. I didn't know it would be so dangerous. I'm sorry. I love you."

I stood up.

"You make me so angry!" I said. "But...."

I didn't finish my sentence. Otter was kissing me and I was kissing him back.

THANK YOU

Thank you for reading A Dangerous Weekend. (Word count: 10,947) We hope you enjoyed it.

If you would like to read more graded readers, please visit our website http://www.italkyoutalk.com

Other Level 3 graded readers include
A Holiday to Remember
Akiko and Amy Part 1
Akiko and Amy Part 2
Akiko and Amy Part 3
Be My Valentine
Different Seas
Enjoy Your Business Trip
Enjoy Your Homestay
I Need a Friend
Old Jack's Ghost Stories from England (1)
Old Jack's Ghost Stories from England (2)
Old Jack's Ghost Stories from Ireland
Old Jack's Ghost Stories from Japan
Old Jack's Ghost Stories from Scotland
Old Jack's Ghost Stories from Wales
Party Time!

Stories for Christmas
The Curse
Together Again
Who is Holly?

ABOUT THE AUTHOR

I Talk You Talk Press is a Japan-based publisher of language textbooks, graded readers and language learning/teaching resources.

Our team is made up of highly experienced language teachers and translators, who have all studied at least one additional language to an advanced level.

This experience enables us to design our materials from the perspective of both the teacher and the learner. We consult with both teachers and language learners when designing our textbooks and graded readers, and test our materials extensively in the classroom before publication.

We are a fast-growing press, and currently publish graded readers for learners of English. We publish new graded readers monthly.

www.ingramcontent.com/pod-product-compliance
Lightning Source LLC
Chambersburg PA
CBHW022345040426
42449CB00006B/735